T0064677

THE
BOOK
OF
OLD

NANCY KNUDSEN

ARCHWAY
PUBLISHING

Credit to Nancy B. Call Knudsen & Jeremy R. Call
Interior Graphics/Art Credit: Nancy B.
Call Knudsen & Jeremy R. Call

Archway Publishing books may be ordered
through booksellers or by contacting:

Archway Publishing
1663 Liberty Drive
Bloomington, IN 47403
www.archwaypublishing.com
1 (888) 242-5904

ISBN: 978-1-4808-5576-2 (sc)
ISBN: 978-1-4808-5577-9 (e)

Library of Congress Control Number: 2017918645

Print information available on the last page.

Archway Publishing rev. date: 12/01/2017

*This book is dedicated to my family and
friends who unknowingly provided many of
the experiences written about in this book.*

*My Husband
Ray*

*Our Children & Spouses
Jim/Anne, Kelley/Kenny, Travis/Whitney,
J.R./Phyliss & Dana/Glen*

*My Grandchildren
Jeremy (My Memory Keeper), Ike,
Danielle, Kelly, Jens & Eric*

All Our Great Grandchildren

*My Sisters and Their Families
Alice & Suzanne*

*My Friends
Linda & Marion*

*A Special Dedication to My Brother Bob Who
Unknowingly Inspired Me to Start This Book.
Also, His Wife Andy and Their Families*

*In Memory of my Parents, Grandparents
and All My Family Who Contributed
to Making Me Who I Am Today*

I Love You All!

Contents

Introduction

This story goes back to 1947, the beginning of the baby boomer generation, and my birth year. For those of you born in the Sixties and beyond, you need to pay close attention to everything you will read in this book, even though you think it doesn't apply to you. It probably will apply at some point in your lifetime.

I will be starting with what happens to you from the time you reach forty until... Until is the one variable to this story because it will depend on the age you were when you started reading this book, the age you are now, and the age you will be when you die.

Now, get ready for some facts about aging that you may or may not have heard about. Be ready to laugh out loud when you realize that most of these facts are what we all will experience in the future if we haven't already!

Just remember one thing, everyone experiences these aging exploits in their own order. What may happen to you at age forty-five may happen to someone else at age fifty. Don't be discouraged; you will get your chance to share these delights of aging in your own good time—unless, of course, you're dead.

Let's not forget the ever-changing world from playing "Buck Rogers and his spaceship" in the crawl space of your home to man landing on the moon and beyond (Please don't ask who Buck Rogers was).

When I first thought about writing this book I was talking to my brother after he had a hip replacement, a fall ten months later that broke his other hip, and an accident just when the broken hip was almost healed. He slipped on a throw rug and broke both bones in his lower leg.

I called him and jokingly said, "Hey, Bob, you didn't read the book, did you?" He questioned me as to what book and I said, *The Book of Old.* Of course, he hadn't heard of this book, but that was because I hadn't written it yet.

I have now decided it is time to write this book and share all phases of growing old with those of you who cannot find a way (other than death) to get out of it. Chapter 1 will start with the big "4-0" because that's when it begins. Remember, whether you're a man or a woman you will now begin the "Cycle of Old." In many ways, it will be the same, but it will also be very different in other ways. BEWARE THE CYCLE OF OLD!

1

Denial

One morning right before your fortieth birthday, you will wake up and realize that you're going to be forty. You look in the mirror and think *Look at me; I look great, not like other people I know who are in their forties.* Then you get specific; John or Joan has started to go gray and look at the weight they've put on. That's not going to happen to me! I take care of myself; I walk, work out and watch what I eat (well, except for when we have dessert or go to the fast food restaurant for their fried chicken. I really love that fried chicken).

So it begins—not all at once but little baby steps that get you in trouble. Now, it may not happen right away, but it will happen! One day you wake up, and it's cold outside, or maybe it snowed last night, and you decide you can't walk today, but you will walk a little longer tomorrow (that ain't happening). Tomorrow, it's colder than today, and the cycle starts.

Even though you can't take that walk, you can still work out, and you will, but now your routine has been thrown off. You will find that in the beginning, Cycle of Old routines are very important and very hard to restart once they get interrupted. Now, without the walk, you have some spare time, so you sit down and watch a little TV. Along with the TV, you need a snack, not a big snack, just something to munch on.

Guess what? That show you were watching was interesting, but with the extra time and the snacks, you fell asleep (or else you were watching it through the pinholes in your eyelids). Once you wake up, you feel a little guilty about not getting enough exercise, but it's dinnertime, and you'll do better tomorrow. This may not happen every day, but it will happen enough to throw your whole routine off, and it becomes a slippery slope to try and get back into your regimen.

As you progress from age forty to forty-five, you will find that when you get home from work, you need a few minutes to rest and relax before you try taking that walk or lifting those weights. You still think you feel just like you did when you were in your thirties, but guess what; that's just a dirty trick your brain is playing on your body. Your body knows better, but your brain is saying *I remember how we did it and I know we can still do it.* (Hey, you just got fooled!!)

Before you know it, you have a little ache in your side, or a muscle pulled in your back, and you are wondering what did I do to cause this pain. The Cycle of Old is just beginning. Embrace it; there will be more!!

Here's a little flip side to the "I walk, work out and watch what I eat" scenario. If you were always an athlete when you were younger, and you played sports like football, basketball, baseball, track, tennis, hockey or any combination of these, then your body has been beat up, abused and otherwise destroyed by the overuse of your knees, hips, shoulders and sometimes even your brain. The flip side is it hurts to walk too far; your shoulders can't bear a lot of weight anymore, and your brain—well, you think it hasn't been affected, but why does it keep telling you that you can still do this when your body says, "No, please no more pain"?

To continue the flip side metaphor in the matter of "I watch what I eat," that's exactly what you did when you were younger. You watched all the foods you enjoyed pile in large portions onto your plate because you never gained a pound. Guess what; it doesn't work that way anymore. Now you watch all the food you enjoy pile up as large portions of fat on your hips, arms, legs and stomach. Welcome again to the Cycle of Old!!

2

Men's Denial and MM

Now, you've probably heard that men age better than women, and in some ways, that's true, but don't believe everything you hear. When a man reaches his forties, he starts looking back at everything he's done. What does he see? What he should see is all that he has accomplished so far in his life, but what he will see is all the things he hasn't done. He is now entering Male Menopause (MM for short).

What does this mean? Well, some men (not all) feel like all they've ever done was work, pay bills and take care of their families. They feel that now it's their turn to do what they want, and they try to go back to what they think they missed out on when they were younger and/or married. Big, big mistake!!

You've probably heard the expression "you can never go back." This is true. They are now in their forties, not eighteen, and not "foot-loose and fancy-free."

Some men will take up or renew a sport that they loved when they were younger. Others will want to show how virile they still are and will start looking at women, especially the younger ones. Now many of these we can call flings, but to the men it means they still "have it," and it becomes a matter of their egos, recapturing their youth and showing the guys how "studly" they still are. (Keep in mind, there are always exceptions. Some men don't even settle down until they are in their forties and are very content in their relationships.)

Very few of these flings last or end well. If they are single, the young women will eventually start looking at younger men, especially as the newness of the relationship wears off. Some of the women will be looking for a father figure, others want financial security and need someone who will cater to their every whim and buy them pretty things. This can get old when the men start to regain their senses as they mature (we can hope).

Some of these men have been married for several years, and when the Cycle of Old takes over, their brains quit working and the last surge of testosterone kicks in. When this happens, there are two solutions: 1) the man can realize that this is a part of the Cycle of Old and not give in to it, or 2) he can give up everything he has ever worked for and everyone that is important to him for a temporary boost to his ego. He should remember new and different isn't always better than experienced and familiar.

The most important lesson that can be learned is that the next woman could be worse than the first. Watch out for what you wish for or what you think you want!! <u>Beware the Cycle of Old.</u>

Now, this is not the only trap MM might bring on. There is the dreaded, "I've always wanted…" syndrome. You ladies know exactly what I'm talking about: I always wanted to fly an airplane; I always wanted to sail around the world; I always wanted to climb Mount Everest, etc. (They better not say they always wanted to marry Suzie Cutie or you may be ready to kill them and claim in court that PMS made you lose control).

There are also many subtle changes that take place with MM, like wanting to tell everyone how to do everything, thinking how stupid people are who don't do the things you like to do, imagining you have symptoms of a disease you just heard about on the news, knowing you can play sports better than the pros and screaming at the TV for a bad play (now this may have been happening all along, and it seems to escalate with age, but it will continue and it will get worse).

There is a lot more I can say about men in their forties and MM, but the fifties and sixties get even better. All I can say is, watch out—as the years pass, each decade brings new and more challenging changes into our men's lives, and believe me, I repeat, <u>it will get worse</u>!!

 **3**

Women's Denial and the Big M

After reading the previous chapter, I hope I haven't misled you about this book. *The Book of Old* is an equal opportunity publication. I will be giving equal time to both men and women at various stages of their lives. Now women take note of what to look for as you enter the world of the big "4-0."

At this point in your life, you are either just beginning menopause (M for short) or have experienced the subtle beginnings of it. You can expect mood swings, the PMS Monster (Monster for short; your husbands should hide when this happens), hot flashes at the most inopportune times, night sweats, sleep disruptions, and best of all the slow but inevitable waning of your monthly visitor (Yeah!!).

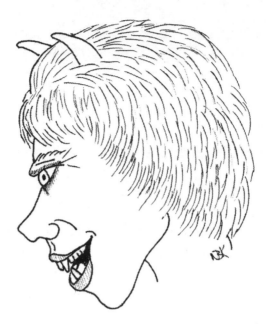

A man's view of the "PMS Monster"

This is the beginning of the best years of your life. How can this be? you ask. Well, think about it: no more monthly visitor, no more worrying about unexpected pregnancies, and by now you should have learned the word "NO" and how to use it to your advantage. You can say to your husband, "NO, I don't want to" (this can be anything and everything), and he will say okay because he doesn't want to see the Monster evolve. Your kids will still get on your nerves, but you can also say NO to them. The only difference is they won't understand about the Monster until it's too late. The bewildered looks on their faces are priceless when you say, "NO, and if you don't like it, there's the door."

A child's view of the "PMS Monster"

We all know you don't really mean you want them to leave but the Monster has taken over your body and your mind, and it is now in control of both. This is the time to be left alone to allow time for the Monster to withdraw into the depths of hell aka PMS.

A teen's view of the "PMS Monster"

I must now address the issue that bothers women the most (even more than the Monster); this is the first gray hair. Although there are some women who go prematurely gray because of heredity factors, illnesses or for unexplained reasons, and these women have already gone through denial, they are the exceptions.

When they realize they are going gray, some women may go into a depression and denial stage. This does not take the graying process away; it's downhill from here. My take on going gray and getting wrinkles is that it's God's dirty little trick. First, your vision starts to go, and you don't see the gray or the wrinkles, and then one day you get GLASSES (another dirty word). Once you put the glasses on and look in the mirror, you find that you don't just have one gray hair but several gray hairs and the same for wrinkles. Every day you look in the mirror, and before you know it, more gray hairs are appearing like magic (black, evil magic, to be precise).

Eureka! Never fear, henna is here; it's a miracle!! Now is the time to start dying, glazing or highlighting your hair. You can now thank God for giving us the technology to stop the Gray Invasion.

But wait, there's more! What about women's bouts with weight gain, especially during M? There is a direct correlation between M and weight gain, so to avoid excess gaining, try to become more active. I know you're saying, "<u>More active?</u> I already get up early to get the kids off to school, let the pets out, pack lunches, plan dinner, go to work, come home, let the pets out again, straighten up the house, wash a load of clothes, start dinner, help the kids with homework, get the kids ready for bed, etc., etc. When am I supposed to be more active and how—in my sleep?"

Prioritize. Use that Monster to help. You already have instilled in everyone that Fear the Monster

Syndrome, so let it work for you! Tell your husband, "No, I'm not going to do everything anymore; you will have to help or else…" Tell the kids, "No, I'm not going to help you do everything; you're old enough to do most of this yourselves, and if you don't like that, there's the door." Here, again, a little Monster intimidation goes a long way. Use it while you still have the Monster in you. Remember, you will become so irritating, they will do anything to keep you quiet.

The other thing women should be careful about as they start the Cycle of Old is that like the men, they have their own egos to deal with. And yes, they still want to be attractive to men, so they can become flirtatious. They can be very content in their marriages, but if they have spent years catering to a husband's needs and whims while ignoring their own needs, there can be a problem. Women, as well as men, must feel good about themselves, and this can only be accomplished if they are content with themselves. To be content with yourself, you must have a part of you that belongs just to you. You can't gain total happiness from someone else; it must first come from inside of you.

Men, pay close attention. If you want a woman to be more agreeable, try doing something you know she likes. Watch out, though, because if you act bored or appear to not enjoy it, she will know this and won't enjoy herself. Her joy, like yours, is very important. During this phase of the Cycle of Old, a woman must experience her own type of joy (aka food for her soul). Without her own type of joy, your life could be miserable, much like your life would be if you never did the things you really enjoyed.

Remember, in their forties, women are seeing the signs of aging, the start of going gray, a few new wrinkles, the fall of the bums and in many cases the title of Grandma. Wow, when did all this happen! The start of the Cycle of Old can be subliminal and very unnerving at first. If not for the change in the monthly visitor, most women would not even recognize this phase. That is, until the Monster raises its ugly head. It will take several visits from the Monster before women realize what is happening. They were sure it was everyone else with the problem and not them.

This is the time for plenty of patience, fortitude and understanding from her family and friends (and that's not easy). Women, please understand that when the Monster is present, you can be a nasty, disagreeable and belligerent person. You will blame everyone else for your mood swings, but it's not usually them. Be patient; it does get better as you near the next cycle, the Liberated Cycle of the fifties. The world better be ready because you will be a new person with an unbelievable attitude. That's an "I don't give a shit" attitude. Let the fun begin!!

4

Men's Eternal Vision and the Fifties

After surviving the forties and MM, now comes the beginning of the fifties and a new attitude. Men begin to see an end in sight to all the years they have worked, and they realize that retirement is a reality and not too far in the future.

They start spending more time thinking about what they are going to do and how they are going to accomplish this on their schedule. Their schedule could be to retire at age fifty-five, sixty, sixty-two or sixty-five—whatever they decide they want. This is the beginning of their Eternal Vision, which is what do they want to do when they retire.

Some men only want to stay home and work around the house and yard. Others want to travel throughout the country. Then there are the men who want to buy a yacht or a sailboat and sail all over the world or fly to different countries. What specifically they want doesn't matter; it's the vision that counts. The vision is what keeps them going. It gives them that feeling of liberation because now a decision has been made.

Once the decision has been made, all hell could break loose, and it wouldn't matter to them. Their attitude has changed because now they don't care as much about their job. Their focus is on their retirement and how soon it will get here.

Okay, does this attitude change affect others? Certainly, it does. Is this man a husband or significant other, is he a father with teenage children or grown adult children, or is he single with no attachments? Now the attitude begins, and there's no stopping it, but it will get on your nerves if you live with him or you're married to him. Like a Boy Scout, "Be Prepared." It will drive you crazy!

Remember, there are ten years in the fifties. This is just the beginning. The next thing that affects men in their fifties is their health. This is the age when they need to pay attention to how they feel and take the time to get regular check-ups. Some men will go to the extreme and think every little ache or sniffle is a major illness. They do this because they are afraid; that's right, I said A-F-R-A-I-D. These men are afraid, afraid that they might die before they can retire and enjoy their Eternal Vision.

If this seems strange or unbelievable, remember, these are men's fifties, and nothing is too unbelievable for this phase of the Cycle of Old. Most men have always tried to have a macho persona, but with the fifties come doubts. They now doubt their own strength, stamina and sex appeal, which threatens their macho persona. Yes, that big, macho hunk of man you have always known and loved goes through the Doubt Phase of the Cycle of Old, and this can be a very scary phase for men to deal with.

Physically, a lot of men will have changes. Some may start in the forties, and others will not happen until the fifties. These changes are either the Gray Invasion or the Bald Eagle. They don't get a choice in the matter; it's either one or the other. When a man starts to go gray, they can look distinguished and mature. (This is very unfair to women who do not look distinguished or mature, they just look OLD.)

The other choice, the Bald Eagle, is harder for men to accept. The hair starts thinning, usually on top, and the hairline recedes, which is somewhat intimidating to most men. Watch out, everyone; here comes the comb-over, which is meant to hide the bald patch on top (as if no one will know what's under the comb-over). Some men just comb the hair to the front to hide the receding hairline.

There is one thing saving men from the embarrassment of going bald, and that's the popular style of shaving the head. Now the Bald Eagle look for most men is acceptable, and once they resign themselves to the fact that shaving is better than the comb-over, their confidence returns.

The other physical change men go through is the loss of muscle mass. This usually starts in the fifties but progresses into the sixties and is very hard for some men to accept. The sags and droops that accompany the loss of muscle is nature's way of slowing men down before they hurt themselves trying to do something they did easily when they were eighteen. Pay attention, men; listen to your body; life after injury is not as much fun as being able to walk and do everyday activities without injuries.

Throughout their lives, most men are usually more selfish about their wants and needs than women. Now in their fifties, as they plan their Eternal Vision, they look at their finances and find that they may not be as financially prepared for retirement as they thought they would be. This may be related to indulging their wants and needs too often in their younger days. It could also just be that family obligations or bad luck prevented them from being able to save as much as they planned. Either way, they are discovering that the vision they had for the next phase of their life needs a financial boost.

Now they are on a mission to spend less, save more and find a way to earn more money. If you live with a man who has just realized that his Eternal Vision is in jeopardy, watch out!! You are next on his list of cutbacks. He will now question every penny you spend, why you are spending it and ask do you really need what you are buying. His life may be in danger if he doesn't stop because you are ready to go ballistic on him.

Don't worry, you are past your Fear the Monster Syndrome, and his life will be spared. You will need to advise him that he will remain in jeopardy unless he wants to meet your fifties alter ego "I Don't Give a Shit." At times, this can really be worse than the Monster, so he had better *back off.*

Chapter 5

Women's Attitudes and Their Fifties

I've talked about men in their fifties and how they have changed with their Eternal Vision. They start focusing on their retirement and become intense about getting there, but they seem to try to control everyone and everything to attain the Vision.

Well, women also change in their fifties, but it's a different type of change... they just don't care anymore. They acquire the I-don't-give-a-shit attitude—Attitude for short. Their families are grown, most of them now have grandchildren, and if they are still working, most of them have experience, knowledge and the respect of their co-workers and superiors. This gives them a special power, the power of confidence.

After being a wife, a mother and/or a working woman for many years, a woman in her fifties now realizes that she is a valuable asset to everyone. This gives her self-confidence, which leads to the new Attitude. She now knows that whatever she does, it will be what is right for her, and no one can tell her any different. If they try, she doesn't care because what are they going to do—fire her, leave her or divorce her? So what; she now knows she is valuable and self-sufficient, and this gives her a special power called Attitude, which she has learned to use to her advantage.

With the Attitude, men can no longer bully her; kids can no longer manipulate her, and at work, they treat her with respect because everyone knows a Woman with Attitude is ferocious and someone to be reckoned with. Please don't misunderstand; she will always be the person you know and love. She just won't care if the house is not perfect or if the kids didn't call and heaven forbid if her husband asks her, "Why?" That's why anything; it just doesn't matter why he is asking why. Better not ask it. She is a Woman with Attitude, and she doesn't feel that she must explain anything to anybody at this time in her life. If you don't believe me, just wait!!!

There are more than attitude changes in women's lives in their fifties, and I will cover many if not all of them. Keep in mind, we are all different, and the changes that people I know and I have experienced may not be the same as what you, the reader, may experience or have experienced. Your changes may be a little different, but the majority of women will experience a lot of what is written about in this book.

Your personality will determine when your changes will take place and what they are. There are several categories of women's personalities that tend to make it harder for them to give in to these changes. Eventually, they will succumb to the changes that fit their personalities. It might take longer for some than for others, but the changes will come, and one day they will wake up and feel liberated and not know why. Hopefully, they will figure it out and understand that they are special and deserve to be themselves and do and say whatever they want without needing to please anyone else.

It is women's nature to be nurturers. This is what they have done for years, but when they reach their fifties, something takes over. They are now possessed, possessed by the "What About Me" and "Now It's My Turn" attitudes. These two attitudes are very powerful for women because they give them permission to love and care for themselves and to start putting their wants and needs first.

I have addressed women's attitudes in their fifties, but there is more going on in this ever-changing decade. Now I will elaborate on the physical and emotional changes that women go through in their fifties that can affect those closest to them.

In the forties, there was the big "M," and fortunately most of us survived unscathed. Now there are things happening to our bodies and minds that are totally unfair. First, we acquire a new best friend, the Ladies Room. You may not consider her your best friend, but if you don't visit her often enough, when the call comes, you may end up having a very embarrassing moment, EM for short. An EM can arrive in many ways: a hearty laugh, a hard sneeze, a simple cough, and don't forget the inevitable idea, "I can wait a little longer." Don't try to wait; you may be S-O-R-R-Y!!

If you are not yet in your fifties, you may not believe this will happen to you. All I can say is, "Ha ha!" The joke's on you because it will happen when you least expect it. If you live long enough, it *will* happen!

Before mentioning more serious issues, I must warn everyone about the "Three Little Pigs" syndrome. Now, if this has already happened to you, you will know right away what I'm talking about. For everyone else, I'll explain this syndrome. As women age, they start to lose estrogen and gain testosterone, which can cause hair growth. Now, this hair growth is never where you would like it to grow but above your lips and on your chinny, chin, chin. Hence the name, "Three Little Pigs" syndrome.

The "3 Little Pigs" with Chin Hair

I remember as a child seeing some of the older women at our family reunions with mustaches and chin hairs. I always wondered what was wrong with them. Now I know. I now have my second new best friend, my tweezers, and you can find them in several rooms of my home as well as my car.

If you're wondering why there are tweezers in various locations, you will find out between your late forties and early fifties. This new and not so wonderful joke the Cycle of Old is playing on you is not soft, barely noticeable hair but coarse, thicker and sometimes (not always) darker, more noticeable hair. You could be anywhere when you reach up to your face and find stubble. One, maybe two new hairs grew in the middle of the night, and you are now on a mission to remove them before someone sees them. You will become possessed by the phobia to remove every unwanted hair on your face.

If this seems improbable or unbelievable, just ask an older female friend. If she is honest, she will confirm the Three Little Pigs syndrome and she, like all of us, won't be happy about it. The Cycle of Old strikes again!

Another health issue that usually starts in your fifties is loss of muscle mass. If you have not been a very active person, this could happen in your forties, but let's pretend you have always been in pretty good shape, and it starts in your fifties. If you work outside the home, have a family and only exercise once or twice a week, you will find that before you know it you will have grown Bat Wings. For those of you who don't know what Bat Wings are, go to the sink in a sleeveless shirt or no shirt, lean over the sink, put your hands on your head and look back under your arms. There they are, your Bat Wings, hanging from the loose skin on your upper arms. "How did that happen?" you will ask yourself. The answer is age and loss of muscle mass.

Prepare yourself, stay active and exercise daily or else those Bat Wings will grow into the dreaded Humongous Bat Wings, and your wings will look like curtains hanging on your arms.

This will happen because, as you age, you require more rest. When you work, take care of your family and home, you are now too tired to exercise as much as you used to. It is too easy to come home from work and take a break or nap before you start doing the household duties that you could breeze through when you were younger. Since you always seem to be tired, exercise is the first thing that gets cut. I call this the "It's my excuse and I'm sticking to it" syndrome. Try to always remember my saying: "If you don't exercise and do strength-building things, don't be surprised when you see your Bat Wings."

All kidding aside, there are some serious health issues that women should be aware of and pay attention to. These are: heart disease, diabetes, strokes, Alzheimer's and osteoporosis. These can be very debilitating, and women should discuss these with their doctors and/or health care providers to help prevent any serious problems. These can occur at earlier ages but they seem to become more prevalent in the fifties.

Chapter 6

The Battle of the Aging

Another issue I want to address is how you deal with a husband or significant other in your fifties. We have discussed the Attitude, but now you are dealing with men in their fifties or sixties with their own attitudes, and that's not easy even with Attitude. We now have two attitudes colliding; the man is used to his wants and needs being most important, and now he's found that his partner expects her wants and needs to be most important. Bam!! What an explosion this could be. Who will come out on top?

If you're a man, you will think the man will come out on top, and if you're a woman, you will think it's the woman. I wouldn't dare try to influence your response on this subject. All I will say is, what happens in your home stays in your home. Just remember the expression, "the truth will set you free" and be honest with yourself about what happens in your home. There is no right or wrong answer to this question. There is only the observation that in relationships, as the Cycle of Old takes over, both men and women can have equal amounts of testosterone and attitude, which at times can cause fireworks.

Recognizing the attitudes of others will help both men and women understand what is going on when the explosion happens. Hopefully, this will ease the tension that arises when attitudes clash and make both parties realize that each is entitled to his/her own opinions and needs.

Now comes the unexpected. What does a woman in her fifties really want to do? She's not too old to have fun, and she's old enough to know how! I'm going to list several choices because different women want different things, and there is no wrong choice. Many women want to stay in the home where they raised their family. Others want to downsize their home but still be near their family and friends as well as their grandchildren. Some want to sell their home and travel with their husband or significant other. There are also women who, as a result of death, divorce or because they have always been single, want to travel with friends or family. Let's not forget, there are some women who still enjoy playing, especially with younger men. I believe they are referred to as Cougars. Whichever of the above choices a woman makes is okay, as long as she is happy with her decision.

Making the decision to do any of the above can be very challenging and is something that does not have to be decided in her fifties. However, she should be making a plan for herself. If she is married, she and her husband should be planning what they want to do together. Right or wrong, they both need to understand that men as well as women are entitled to the happiness that can only come from within themselves. Without this inner happiness, a part of them is missing, and this can affect relationships.

The hardest part of The Cycle of Old is learning about yourself and understanding how to take care of yourself while still taking care of others. This is necessary before the sixties because the sixties for both men and women are very scary and challenging. The sixties can be life- changing for everyone; that decade is the beginning of a whole new phase of The Cycle of Old, the downhill side of the Cycle. This cycle should be embraced by all because it is the beginning of our Last Hurrah in the best way. If you're wondering what can make the Last Hurrah great, read on; there is more, and it can be fun and very revealing to the younger set.

7

Men's Sixties: The Vision Begins

Picking up from Chapter 4 and the "Eternal Vision," the sixties is when the vision begins for men. The early sixties is now the countdown phase, and the euphoric feelings begin to slowly take over as men close in on their Eternal Vision. At sixty-three and a half, they realize that they now have only eighteen months until they are sixty-five and can retire. Oh, but wait a minute, they now find that there was a change in the Social Security law and they can't draw their full Social Security until they are sixty-six, so they decide to wait another year.

What do you think happens to them now? Well, their first reaction is disappointment and disgust. Then comes anger. How can this be? I've worked hard all my life, been a good husband, father and provider, and now I'm supposed to work longer than my father had to work. It's not fair!!!

Now is the time for the woman to be the voice of reason. She needs to explain that he now has one more year to save money, to finalize his plans for retirement and to tweak that Eternal Vision so it is exactly the way he wants it to be before he quits work.

He is still disappointed, but he buys into the rationale presented to him, and he seems to settle down for now. Watch out; disappointment can cause strange reactions. Now he is obsessed with the countdown, and he may be very hard to live with, almost impossible. He is becoming the Beast and thinks that if he didn't have the house/rent payment, if the electric bill wasn't so high, if they didn't owe the credit cards, they could retire anyway.

"The Beast"

This is the time to approach him with the idea of the List. The List is what will give him focus and with focus comes a calming of the Beast. This is a distraction—a good distraction for his disappointment. The List should cover everything needed to accomplish his goal. It must be in chronological order. Having dates by when each action to achieve his goal will be accomplished makes it easier to maintain the focus needed to keep the Beast in check until the goal is reached. It is also a gauge or measurement as to how long it should take before his Eternal Vision becomes a reality. He may also find that he thinks of more things he wants to put on the list that hadn't occurred to him before he started his list.

After the list is complete, it is time to immediately start doing and crossing off whatever is on that list. If you are a man who doesn't like lists, don't be afraid! It won't bite, bark or cause you any physical pain, but it will help keep you on point to reach your vision totally prepared to begin your retirement journey.

Keep in mind, the list might include things that need to be done that are work-related, financial, physical and emotional. Let's elaborate on each one of these items that may be on your list or that you may want to add to your list. (Just a note, making a list is also suggested for women who are waiting to retire. They can use the same items.)

Work-related: 1) picking a date; 2) notifying Human Resources or your boss; 3) contacting Social Security with your retirement date and setting up Medicare; 4) picking a supplemental insurance program; 5) checking the dates and times all paperwork needs to be signed and turned in to both Human Resources as well as Social Security; 6) clearing out all personal information from your work area; 7) completing any jobs you may be working on or making a list of what needs to be done for your replacement.

Financial: 1) making sure you have enough combined income from your retirement, Social Security, savings, IRA's and any other sources (such as part-time work, hobbies, or emergency funds) to live comfortably until you die; 2) depending on your plans, either paying off your home, selling it or downsizing; 3) planning your will, estate or appointing who in your family can access your accounts if you need assistance.

Physical: 1) clean and downsize your closets, garages, basements and storage areas; 2) throw out all excess items you don't use; 3) prepare your yard for low maintenance; 4) if you have any new physical challenges and live in a multi-level home you may want to move to a one-level home, apartment or condo with no maintenance or outdoor upkeep.

Emotional: 1) if you do have to move from a home you have lived in and raised a family in for many years it will be an emotional challenge; 2) you will also have the loss from the deaths of family, friends and even pets that will be hard to deal with. Your list can include a time frame for everything except the emotional losses that will occur as you age. These are not to be included on your list.

So now the list is complete and the man can start working on checking off the items as he completes them. How does he feel now? He should start feeling good because he now has control of preparing his life for after retirement. We all know that men love to be in control and have some structure in their lives.

This can be one of the best things to happen to men...UNLESS...yes, I said unless they try to control other people. Those other people would probably be their wives or significant others. That could cause major problems. I want everyone to understand that I know there are many men who are sweet, and not controlling. I am not putting the entire male population into the controlling category; I am just pointing out what can happen to men under stress. Therefore, men, make the plan, make the list and try to follow it. You will be happier because you will have a compass to follow into retirement. Now the Beast will be calmed because he has focus and he knows he is headed in the right direction.

Always remember, the Beast could raise his ugly head at any time in the future if things change and roadblocks appear. That will be when you realize that you can add detours to your plan. A life plan is only as good as its flexibility, and yes, as you age, you better remain flexible. Life has a way of providing us with surprises, and they can be good or unpleasant ones. Protect yourself, beat the Beast, be prepared! Be sure your plan is flexible and has options built in!!!

Chapter 8

Men's Sixties Continued— His Change of Life

Now that a man has prepared his plan, and retirement has arrived, there will be changes that occur in his everyday life. This is the Interim Period, IM for short, which is the time after he retires but before he starts his Eternal Vision.

This is a time when a man, by choice, no longer has a career. The problem is that men never realized how important their careers were in defining who they are. Without their jobs, they need to find something else that will give them the satisfaction and importance that they got from their careers. Here it comes, Mr. Know Everything. (s.a.)!!

This is one of the most challenging moments in a relationship and one of the hardest for two people to deal with. No matter how much a man wanted to retire, a piece of him is now missing. Until he is ready to take the journey of the Eternal Vision, what does he do with himself? He doesn't just jump from retiring from his job into the Eternal Vision; there will be a transition period.

I'll tell you what he will do during this period; he will drive you crazy!! With time on his hands, he starts getting involved with your household daily activities. As if that's not bad enough, now he starts telling you how to do things. He actually thinks he knows how to do things better in the short time he's been retired than you know after spending twenty/thirty years doing the same things day after day. He now has the "I can build a better mousetrap" syndrome and you are stuck with this until you can figure out how to get him out of your world and out of the house. Ask many older women who are still working why they are still working. Most will say that since their husbands retired, they had to keep working or else…

You can encourage him to do the things he loves or to try something new, but even if he does try, it won't last long. This is when he needs to be reminded of the List. Remember, the list is supposed to keep him focused and heading in the direction of the Eternal Vision and away from your world. It is imperative to both the mental and physical health of a man's spouse or significant other for him to have direction, focus and a good working plan to follow after retirement. Men, if you love your spouse or significant other, never forget your List. If you think you don't need one, then at least make one for her sake. I promise, life *will be* more pleasant!!!

Let's now look at the list: 1) has he even made it or just said he did; 2) if he has made one, has he made any attempt to follow it; 3) did he specify dates in order to reach the goals within a reasonable time; 4) were the goals realistic and attainable or just bull s--- to make the woman happy; 5) does he have to be reminded of the list and then says "it will get done"; and 6) does he make excuses constantly as to why the list won't work.

If any of the above applies to your man, then you have a big problem!! If you have a man who refuses to use the list, then you may be in trouble. Now, a man in his sixties and recently retired who won't use a list is called a TYRANT. He thinks he knows more than everyone else and is going to prove it by *not* trying anything anyone else suggests. This is when a wife or significant other must get creative if the relationship is to survive because her man won't try new things or won't even be receptive to new ideas.

The question now is how to motivate this type of man and why is he being so uncooperative? The answer could be as simple as he may be going through another change of life and experiencing a mild depression or a feeling of withdrawal from his former life. Remember, if this is the case, patience can only go so far to help him overcome this mood. So, what can a woman do? If she gets mad and loses her patience, it really won't help; it will just cause her blood pressure to go up and her attitude to change. (If she's not careful, The Monster will return.)

The next best solution is to ignore him and go about your own business and enjoy yourself. Do the things you like and have always wanted to do, but be sure you plan and have a daily list of all the things you're going to do. If you go somewhere, have fun and always come home in a good mood but don't volunteer any information. Only elaborate on what you did if he asks, and eventually, he will ask. If he doesn't ask right away, then do things around the house you like doing and be happy! Eventually, curiosity will get the best of him, and he will ask where have you been and what have you been doing. Remember, he is the one who knows how to do everything better than anyone else and wants to tell everyone how to do things. Now is the time to tell him, "I had a few things on my list I had to take care of today and surprisingly, I had a good time doing them."

Don't volunteer any more information than that; just make sure you have something to do on your list every day. If he asks you to do something for him, you can tell him you won't have time because you have things to do. He may or may not get the hint of what you're doing, but it will get him thinking about things he could be doing. Once he decides that sitting around the house by *himself* is no fun, maybe he will figure out that he could do more things now that he's retired and have fun!

Remember, depending on the man, this method may get results in a short time, or it might take longer than you want. The change of life doesn't happen overnight so don't expect it to necessarily improve overnight. (The challenge is on!!!)

Wait, the fun is just beginning!! Everyone seems to think that aging happens to all of us and that it is simply the next phase of our lives, much like the ones before it, at least in terms of relationships. I want everyone to know that it's a bit more complicated; when you live with a spouse or significant other, you still love each other, but there is something unexpected that happens. It's called The Battle of the Aging. As you read this book, pay close attention to the differences in aging that happen to men and women. As you read on, you will see how different men and women accept, deal with and embrace The Final Phase.

Chapter 9

What Do Women Really Want in Their Sixties?

If you happen to be around a woman in her sixties, don't, I repeat, DON'T, try to figure her out or think you know what she wants. No matter what you think, it *will* be wrong. Do you know why it will be wrong? It's because she doesn't know for sure what she really wants.

This is a major transition in her life, and to her, it feels like the beginning of the end. Try making a list of all the changes that she has seen in the last thirty years. 1) For most women, turning thirty was the first time that the feeling of getting old entered their minds. This was a passing moment for some women, while for others it was a major milestone. 2) In their forties, they had the big M, the Monster, the Gray Invasion, the start of wrinkles and the need for glasses. These could be totally demoralizing. 3) Then, in their fifties, they got the Attitude, their New Best Friend and the Three Little Pigs Syndrome.

With all the changes she has been through, it's no wonder she doesn't know what she wants. Her life has changed completely from that carefree young woman who had great plans for her life and a dream of how it was supposed to turn out. She now looks back at her life and realizes that it wasn't exactly like she thought it would be.

In her sixties, a woman goes through many emotional changes: her children have grown up and have their own families, and she no longer feels needed in their lives; her home and her heart feels empty without the kids; if she had a career, it's coming to an end, and even though it will be nice not to have to go to work every day, she will miss her friends and her routines; and lastly, if she has a husband or significant other, there will be an adjustment period. Without their careers to occupy their time, they will now be together constantly. Unless they can find their own hobbies and interests, this can be emotionally draining and the start of The Battle of the Aging.

"The Battle of the Aging"

Pay close attention to the women you know who either quit their jobs early or retired with a spouse or significant other at home. Now look at how many either went back to work full time or got a part-time job to get out of the house. In most cases, this was done to avoid the Battle of the Aging.

Now, there are the physical changes that have been pointed out to me by women like myself who are now over sixty. I have a friend who brought to my attention that, years ago, as children, we were given a smallpox vaccine that left a scar on our upper arm. She told me that hers is no longer on her upper arm but is now just above her elbow. When I told this to a man I know who for years worked out with weights, he laughed and shared with me that his scar is now around the back of his arm. (BEWARE:

when you stop using your muscles as much as you did when you were younger the muscle will shrink [atrophy], and the skin from around that muscle will travel, with the help of gravity, downward. This causes more sagging skin, wrinkles and exaggerated Bat Wings.) Welcome to the sixties, ladies!!

Women in their sixties, who are going through the Battle of the Aging with their spouses, will also suffer from the lesser known syndrome that I call the Tick-Tock, Tick-Tock, You're Running out of Clock syndrome. This usually happens in the late sixties, and it comes from the changes in their relationships with their family and friends. They feel like they don't have enough time left to do everything they have always wanted to do.

Also, as people age, they tend to have less energy, which makes for less time to devote to relationships outside their immediate families. Now, without them quite realizing it, there is a loss in their lives. This affects women more than men because women are communicators, and their friends have always been their lifelines. A woman's friends are the ones they have always talked to about life, kids, relationships, work and anything else that may bother them. Many times, they can open up and share their feelings with a friend about things they feel they can't share with a spouse or significant other.

The loss can be a result of friends moving away, retiring and not being as easily available, or dying. No matter why they are no longer around, a woman will feel the loss of her friends and not even realize that it is bothering her.

Remember, many couples can share almost everything with each other, but they are the exceptions. There is nothing wrong with either way as long as the women can share their feelings with someone to help relieve the stresses in their lives. There is something important that couples must remember to do when sharing their feelings with each other. That is to Listen to what they are saying, Accept their feelings, Say nothing critical and Trust the love they share (L.A.S.T.).

Always try to remember this acronym, LAST. It can ease the Battle of the Aging and help both to better understand each other. The acronym LAST should also help both men and women make their relationships last and grow stronger!

After the loss of her friends, she may still not be able to share all her feelings with her spouse or significant other. This is the time for her to break out the New Me persona. She needs to join clubs, functions or activities that provide her with things she is interested in and new friends she can share things with. This will be addressed more in Chapter 12.

Women have always been strong. This strength manifests in raising their families, taking care of a home, for many while holding down a job, in some cases taking care of sick or elderly parents, and—not to be forgotten—loving the children and grandchildren. Because they are strong, women will be able to survive this Battle of the Aging as long as they have the inner strength and happiness to feel good about themselves.

It doesn't matter if you are a man or a woman. What matters is how you feel about yourself and not how you think someone else feels about you! Always be true to yourself. Do not become an extension of a spouse or significant other or you will never be truly happy. Develop what I call the Popeye Syndrome: I am who I am. When you know who you are and like who you are you will be happy!

Happiness will help you overcome the challenges you face as you go through the Cycle of Old and it will help you win the Battle of the Aging. Just follow your heart, love yourself first, and the transition into the Final Phase of the Cycle of Old will be unbelievable!!

Chapter 10

The Seventies, the Men, and How They Survive

Men, don't panic, if you've survived the sixties, then you probably are pretty darn healthy for your age! You may have had some health issues through the fifties and sixties, but you have reached the seventies none the worse for wear.

This is the age when you are paying attention to your health, watching what you eat and pacing yourself in your activities. This is a big plus because these things are known to extend your life expectancy. We all know that the most important thing to a person in their seventies is the question, "How much longer do I have?"

Well, the answer to that question, as discussed in the Introduction to this book, varies. No one knows how long he or she will live. Remember, now that you accept your age, you are paying close attention to everything you do. For example: 1) you watch where you go, being careful not to trip and fall; 2) you take walks to stay active; 3) you take more naps to get through the day; 4) you go to the doctors for regular check-ups to be sure all is well with your health; 5) you don't go out much at night (you don't see so well at night, and you may have some hearing loss), and 6) you go to bed early because you can't stay awake as late as you used to.

Now you ask, "Where is the fun in my life?" There is no one-size-fits-all answer to this question because everyone has a different idea as to what fun is in his life. Here it comes, the answer to the man's question is, "What do you consider fun?" Guess what, he doesn't really know because his wants and needs have changed in the Final Phase of life.

He may think it is some material thing, but in the seventies, it's not always material things that make life fun anymore. Sure, men think that their toys are what makes life fun, but the golf clubs, the motorcycle, the car, the boat, the camper, the Cessna and anything else they might want will not be as much fun as it used to be.

Here it comes, another list! However, this list is not another To Do list but a Here's What I Did Today List. This list is of things that happen almost daily and which, after they are completed, make men feel good. 1) They wake up in the morning and are still alive; 2) they complete their morning constitution, then shower and shave; 3) they eat a healthy breakfast without having acid reflux; 4) they watch TV and the news without having a heart attack over something they disagreed with; 5) they take a drive to get out of the house, maybe stopping at the store; 6) they eat lunch while watching TV, maybe nodding off during their show; 7) they may take a walk after a nice dinner and then; 8) they go to bed by 9 p.m., watch some more TV and fall asleep in the middle of a show. This is life as they know it now, and the purpose of this change is to help conserve energy in case they want to play with a toy.

You can see this is not a bad list at all, and it did not require playing with any toys to make men feel good. This list is a gauge for what makes them happy every day. In the seventies, being able to do all the above without any unpleasant repercussions is considered a Good Day. As stated above, this does not rule out their toys; their toys are still an important part of who they are. However, playtime with their toys has become limited due to their physical condition and energy levels. As they soon discover, the brain is cooperating, so the desire is still there, but the body is arguing and limiting what they can accomplish. This brain/body battle also applies to more than just the toys listed above.

What men can still enjoy are a loving wife or significant other, an extended family with children, grandchildren, maybe even great grandchildren, great friends, a nice home, good food and yes, some of their toys.

As for the Battle of the Aging for men, there will be more arguments and disagreements with the spouse or significant other. When his hearing, vision and health start to fail, his disposition changes also. He may become short-tempered, disagreeable and belligerent because he may think other people say things that they didn't say; he is not seeing things that are clear to others; and he won't admit that there is anything wrong with his hearing, vision or health.

This not only happens to men in their seventies; it can happen to women too. Can you imagine the Battle of the Aging when both live together? This can be chaos because they are not able to communicate with one another in a way that doesn't cause an argument. There will be one person saying, "I said…" and then the other one saying, "No, you did not say that, you said…"

Men, especially, become grumpy, loud and will try to talk over the women. The women become defensive and catch their own Attitude. Now the battle is on!!

This can all be avoided if both parties take care of themselves, get their hearing and vision checked and admit that they have a problem. Now they can take appropriate measures to correct the vision and/or hearing. Once you become aware of your problems and correct them, then the final phase of The Cycle of Old can be embraced as another step of the cycle of life.

Men may ask, "What part of the final phase of the Cycle of Old can I look forward to?" The answer is simple; you are alive, you have lived a full life with family and friends who love and care about you, and you have seen many changes in the world over the last seventy years. Just imagine what the next ten or twenty years will bring if you remember to look at those upcoming years as a new adventure in your life!

This new adventure can include doing anything you love and enjoy as long as your health permits. Some men change their activities from the very physically active ones to the milder and less active ones. Examples could be: swimming, playing cards, photography, drawing & painting, fishing, golf while using a golf cart, walking or walking the dog, traveling, woodworking, etc.

Most of the above can be done every day. The outdoor activities will be weather-permitting activities. You may also decide to go fishing in the morning, paint pictures in the afternoon and play cards in the evening. The choice is yours, and you may find that the list above does not include some of the things you really love. This is where you have options of things you love to do, and you can modify which ones you do every day. The choice is yours because life in your seventies is all about you and the fun you can still have doing the things you didn't have time for when you were younger.

Wow, life can be a dream and not just at seventeen! Relax and enjoy, this is your time to have fun!!

 **11**

For Women—
Let the Seventies Begin

Having just reached the Seventies Milestone, I want to discuss my take on what to expect over the next several years. This will not be based only on personal experience but include information I have received from other women in their seventies. So, let's begin!

First, if you were a conscientious worker at a job from which you have recently retired, then you are going to go through what I call the Withdrawal Phase. When you wake up in the morning, this phase consists of the following questions: "What day is it?"; "What am I supposed to do today?"; "What should I do first?"; "What do I want to watch on TV today?"; "What do I want to eat for lunch?"; "What did I come in this room for?" etc., etc.

You see, without the routine that was a part of your life for many years, your brain and body are now rebelling. Routines make your life work on automatic, and when the routines end, your body does not know how to act or what to do.

Your brain struggles to focus on the changes in your life and sometimes, without focus, you won't remember what you did two minutes ago much less what you want to do next. I have always thought of my brain as a large file cabinet. As you age, you need to empty the old files that you don't use anymore. This is necessary to make room for the new files you need to put in your file cabinet. These files are anything and everything that you have learned throughout your life.

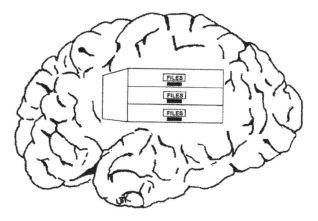

"The File Cabinet in Your Brain"

Everyone seems to think that as you get older, you forget more. Wrong. It's not that you forget more, it's that you don't have any more room in your file cabinet to file what needs to be remembered. For those of you who are younger and don't buy into my theory, just wait!! Unless your brain develops a computer with a flash drive instead of a file cabinet, then this will eventually happen to you too. That's right, believe it or not, unless you're dead, you will get old, and if your file cabinet is full, you too will have trouble remembering.

You don't have to worry because this can work to your advantage. Even when you remember things, you don't have to acknowledge that you remember them. There will be times when it's easier just to say, "I don't remember that" than to get into an argument with someone over something they think you said. This can also be used in reverse. If someone says, "You didn't tell me that!" you can just say, "Yes I did, you must have forgotten." If this person is in their sixties or seventies, they won't be sure because they, like yourself, have had lapses of memory in the past, and they will now question themselves. Life can be a little scary when you really don't remember something, and you start questioning your own memory and sanity.

Trust yourself; you can't remember everything and no one can. If you are busy and concentrating on something, you may not pay attention to everyday things that you do automatically. Common examples would be, where did you put your car keys and why can't you find your glasses (sometimes they may be around your neck or on top of your head). Don't panic, everyone goes through this, and it has nothing to do with their memory (or yours). This usually is caused by overload, trying to do too much at one time and preoccupation with other things.

Relax, this does not mean that you have Alzheimer's or dementia. It just means that you are slowing down and need more rest. After all, you are in your seventies now, and adjustments need to be made. Now is the time to make new routines. Keep in mind that the loss of your routines will affect you in a new way in the Withdrawal Phase. The new routines should now be for fun things, not housework or chores.

Let's not forget the other reason your brain is on overload. You are now at home with your spouse or significant other, and usually he is the same age as you or older. You now suffer from Repeat-itis, which is the constant need to repeat yourself because someone doesn't hear, isn't listening or refuses to listen, especially when you ask them to do something. Refusing to listen has probably been going on for years, but now it is extremely aggravating because you no longer have the energy to constantly be repeating yourself.

Now, you are ready to explode, but let's hope you know better. You need to be careful because this could cause a major rise in your blood pressure and that's not the safest thing to happen to you in your seventies! Take a deep breath, count to ten and calmly ask him, "What did you think I said?" Don't be surprised if he doesn't know exactly what you said. This is the time when you quietly say to him, "Listening is a form of showing you love me. Please try a little harder to show me that you still love me."

Depending on how stubborn your man is, this may or may not work. What it will do is keep you from becoming more stressed, and that is more important than winning the Battle of the Aging. If this does not help, then your second option is to turn the tables on him and not pay attention when he is talking to you. Childish as this may seem, it may be the only way for him to get the point. Good luck!!

 **12**

Stress Relief and How Women Can Survive the Seventies

Let's discuss what you need to do to help relieve the stress involved in the Battle of the Aging. As mentioned in Chapter 9, it is now time to develop other activities. The New Me persona is about to arrive in full force for women.

Here it comes! Women may have already joined a club in their sixties, but in their seventies, it has become an obsession. There's the Garden Club, the Red Hat Club, the Book Club, the Art Center, the Country Club and a variety of volunteering opportunities for her to become involved in.

Don't, I repeat don't, try to influence her in any way to scale down the number of activities she is involved in. She will realize, on her own, that she has taken on too much, and she will then scale down her New Me persona. Any suggestions from anyone else, especially a spouse or significant other, would only cause her stress level to rise and evoke a negative reaction. (You don't want to invite the Temper Troll to rise to the service because it won't be pretty. It could even be worse than the Monster!).

Another thing that women often don't realize is that as they age, there is no compass to life. This was never a topic discussed at the dinner table. In the past, conversation about aging was almost taboo. Something mothers never shared with their daughters when they had the Mother-Daughter talk about life. They discussed the transition from a child to a young lady, sex, marriage and having babies but never discussed the Cycle of Life and getting old.

This is not meant to put blame on anyone; I only want to point out how important it is to understand about aging. Once you understand aging, it will be easier to accept aging. If this were a military issue, you would know that it is important to know your enemy. In this case, aging is the enemy.

I have a friend who recently pointed out to me that she feels lost because she does not know what to expect as she gets older. This made me start thinking, analyzing and documenting the last forty-plus years of life. Life, like a ship, must have a compass, a course and a reason for the journey.

13

Life, a Ship and the Cycle of Old

What do these three things have in common? Well as mentioned at the end of Chapter 12, life is like a ship. In the Cycle of Old, you need the same three ingredients to reach your destination as a ship needs to complete its voyage. These three things are the compass, the course and the journey.

The Book of Old can now be your compass showing the direction you should follow in life as well as many of the roadblocks you will encounter throughout your life. Always remember, just because you have a compass does not guarantee that you won't get lost. If you get lost along the way, go back to your compass (*The Book of Old*) and find where you went off track and modify your course.

Your course is the goal you set for yourself and the plan you made to get there. You may encounter roadblocks or get lost along the way. It may be a little scary not knowing where you are going. That's why your journey is so important. It is what happens to you while you are traveling on your course. It also shows how long the course takes to get you to your destination. In case you're wondering, the reason for your journey is your accomplishments, your family and your legacy.

At the end of the Cycle of Old, all three ingredients will have led you to this wonderful destination. What destination? The first thought that comes to mind for many people is that the destination is death. While death is the inevitable, it is not necessarily the destination.

Whether you are a man or a woman does not matter. The destination will be the same. You travel through life looking for everything you think will make you happy. Many people think that happiness will come if they have lots of money, fame, or the toys they always wanted. If this was the case, how come so many famous people with millions of dollars use drugs, abuse alcohol and have trouble with relationships?

The answer is simple; happiness cannot be bought, borrowed or sold. Believe it or not, for adults, unlike children, it must be earned, and it's not easy because so many people don't really know what will make them happy. In case you missed the sections of this book that referenced that happiness must come from within yourself, please read them again.

Now think; if you love music, doesn't singing and listening to it make you happy? How about art? Does drawing, sketching, painting, carving and sculpting make you happy? Even your children and grandchildren are a part of who you are because they are genetically part of you. Think of the things, not the toys, that make you happy. Whether you are a man or a woman, aren't the things you love a part of who you are and what makes you happy?

Here is the most important thing you should remember: when the part of you that makes you happy becomes the part of you that is the real you, then you have succeeded in having Inner Happiness. Once you have achieved Inner Happiness, dealing with life becomes easier and dealing with the Cycle of Old is no longer as scary or intimidating as originally expected. You should now realize that this is the real destination of the Cycle of Life.

Now you understand that the spouse or significant other who drove you crazy and had a way of getting on your nerves was not the real problem to achieving happiness. The real problem was and is your inner self. You must nurture yourself and allow Inner Happiness to be the very essence of who you are.

Through all the years and changes that happen to both men and women, somehow life goes on. Surprisingly, it goes on without any major incidents, and for the most part, neither the spouse nor significant other can be blamed if a man or a woman has not found their Inner Happiness.

If you're lucky, both you and your spouse or significant other can enjoy a lot of the same things. You can share your moments together doing the things you both enjoy while still holding on to your love and passion for what gives you Inner Happiness. It can take years for two people to figure this out, and both must be selfish about their own Inner Happiness as well as unselfish about the other's need for Inner Happiness.

One thing most couples have in common as they embrace the Cycle of Old is their family, their children and grandchildren. No matter what else gives you Inner Happiness, nothing else will be more important to both of you than the Inner Happiness you receive from the people you raised and nurtured. This is what makes life in the seventies and beyond worth living for.

If you happen to be single, you also need to achieve that same Inner Happiness. Again, only you can find it, and you only need to look within yourself to locate it.

 **14**

Memories, The Final Chapter

Whether you are a man or woman, you should have some wonderful memories in those file cabinets in your brain. So what will happen to all those memories now that you are in your seventies and beyond?

Maybe you better make a plan as to what you are going to do with those memories. Are you going to sit down every evening and reminisce about the past? Will you sit around when your friends come over and tell the same stories over and over again?

I'm sure everyone knows someone between forty and eighty years old who always tells the same stories. (I call them their war stories). Unless they are talking to a new audience who has never heard the stories before, listeners will be polite, but probably get bored after hearing the same story again and again.

I'm not sure if this is because as we age, we aren't doing as many exciting and interesting things as we did when we were younger. An alternative thought is that we just aren't having as much fun since we got older, so we're not making as many good memories.

Whatever the reason, those memories need to be passed on to the family Memory Keeper. Every family should have at least one person who is interested in their family history and wants to know all about their family, their extended family and their ancestors as far back as can be remembered by the past Memory Keepers.

It's hard to imagine that life can still be great when you reach this point in your life. What makes it great is all the memories that you cherish, the family members who love you and who you love. This is what makes the Final Phase of life the Greatest Finale of life. You have completed your journey and reached your destination.

Now, enjoy all your accomplishments and your legacy, which will last even after you're gone!

Please pass on your memories so they can be treasured by future generations of your family. Make sure you have a Memory Keeper who will pass on the memories to the next generation.

At the end, I have a saying, *Memories Are Special Treasures When Passed On To Those Who Follow.*

People say, "Life is worth living." I say, "Life is for living" and we should all be glad we had the opportunity to live it!

We should thank the Cycle of Old for allowing us to complete the Cycle of Life! This is our Last Hurrah, and if you embrace it, you will achieve the best life has to offer: happiness with no regrets.